CAN YOU BELIEVE IT?

A YOUNG PERSON'S GUIDE TO
CONFIRMATION IN THE ANGLICAN CHURCH
STUART THOMAS

Kevin Mayhew

First published in 1997 by
KEVIN MAYHEW LTD
Rattlesden
Bury St Edmunds
Suffolk IP30 0SZ

0 1 2 3 4 5 6 7 8 9

ISBN 086209 962 5
Catalogue No 1500091

Front cover by Eddy Mooney
Cartoons by Fred Chevalier
Edited by David Gatward
Typesetting by Louise Hill
Printed and bound in Finland by
WSOY – Book Printing Division

CONTENTS

FOREWORD   5

BECOMING A PERSON   9

WHAT HAPPENS AT BAPTISM   13

DECISION TIME   17

CAN YOU BELIEVE IT?   23
   Do you believe and trust in God
      the Father who made the world?   24
   Do you believe and trust in his Son,
      Jesus Christ, who redeemed
      humankind?   27
   I believe and trust in the Holy Spirit,
      who gives life to the people of God 30

PERSONAL BELONGING   35
   We come to God with our praise   38
   We come to God with our sins and
      weaknesses   38
   We come to God with our gifts   41
   We come to God with our thanks   42
   We come to God with our prayers   44
   We come to God with our commitment   44

ACTIVE SERVICE   47
   Discipleship   49
   Worship   52
   Fellowship   54
   Stewardship   55
   Leadership   56

LOOK ALIVE   59
  Relationships   60
  At school or college   62
  Opinions   63
  Evangelism   64
  Conflict   65

THE LIFE-SUPPORT SYSTEM   69
  Reading the Bible   70
  Talking to God – and listening   72
  Ideas for approaching prayer   76

THE CONFIRMATION SERVICE   79
  Approaching Confirmation   79
  The four elements of the Confirmation   84
  The significance of the service   87

A QUESTION OF FAITH   89

TAKE THE PLUNGE   93

FOREWORD

Whether or not you want to tell your friends about it, you've reached a point in your life where you're thinking about being confirmed. There are several reasons why this might be. Perhaps you've been thinking about the Christian faith for some time and it's started to make sense to you. Maybe your friends go to church because they've found it's important to them, and you feel you want to belong there too. Quite probably you feel you want to receive the bread and wine at Communion, even if you can't quite put your finger on why. Possibly you've not really thought seriously about your beliefs until now, and someone else has persuaded you to. Whatever the motivation, you're considering whether or not you should be confirmed into the Anglican Church.

Unfortunately it's not really 'cool' to admit you are interested in Christianity. People don't talk very readily about their personal beliefs, and society generally works on the basis that 'it doesn't really matter what you believe so long as you're sincere'. But the Christian faith is expressed both in word and action – if it's the genuine article then you can't help noticing it. When you're confirmed you are making a public statement both about what you believe and how you're intending to live from now on. The Confirmation Service isn't an end in itself – just a vital staging post on your spiritual journey. Being confirmed involves far more than one church service, and you'll need more than a guide book to tell you about it:

1. You need to know what it means to become and then be a Christian, and to think about Baptism, whether or not you've already been baptised, because

part of Confirmation involves remaking your baptismal promises.

2. Those promises form the basis of the creed, so it's important to reflect on what you believe as a Christian – even if you don't understand it fully, now's the time to start!

3. You need to recognise the importance of receiving the bread and wine at the Eucharist.

4. You need to think about what it means to live the Christian life now you've nailed your colours to the mast.

5. Now you're part of the Christian church you'll need to discover your place in it.

6. Your survival as a Christian will depend on you developing good habits of reading the Bible and praying.

If you reckon that's a tall order, then you're absolutely right! But no one ever said Christianity was a soft option. If you want to escape from reality for a while or fancy an easy time, forget it. It's demanding and tough, but utterly fulfilling.

This book isn't a complete D.I.Y. Confirmation kit. Your local vicar or curate will take responsibility for preparing you, and this book is designed to be part of that, by giving you a framework to help you understand better what it means to be confirmed. Don't be afraid to ask questions; even if the answers aren't straightforward, thinking them through will help you grow spiritually.

BECOMING A PERSON

Aunt Mabel was paying her annual visit to the Brown family. Everyone knew exactly what she'd say, and were well prepared for the usual questions. The first one was aimed at five-year-old Katie. 'My goodness, haven't you grown since I saw you last! And what do you want to be when you're grown up?' Katie was ready for this one. 'Rich,' she replied. In case this wasn't clear enough she added sagely, 'Married to a millionaire who'll buy me lots of things.' It wasn't quite the answer Aunt Mabel was expecting but it was true enough for Katie at that point in her life. The question was really about her future career, but at five years old Katie hadn't yet given this too much thought. Perhaps in three years' time she'll have ideas about being a supermodel, an actress or a pop artist. It'll take at least three or four years after that before she starts to think of being a doctor, a lawyer, a teacher or a company director.

Unfortunately there's a world of difference between *becoming* and *being*. Before you can be a doctor you have to pass some very tricky exams and prove you've learnt about the human body and how to put it right. Only when you've become a doctor after years of training can you be a doctor day by day. Even then, there's always something new to learn and more experience to be gained.

Life is a non-stop process of becoming. A baby soon becomes a toddler; the toddler then develops into a schoolchild, and before long a teenager emerges on the scene. Even when the teenager has become an adult, it doesn't stop. Two single people become a married couple, then parents, and later on grandparents. We can't stop it happening any more than King Canute could stop the tide coming in.

You don't need any qualifications or special

training to be confirmed, other than having been baptised. That may well have happened when you were too young to remember, although more and more people are now baptised when they're older. It doesn't make the slightest difference, because as part of the Confirmation Service you're asked by the Bishop to repeat the baptismal promises, confirming what you believe and how you mean to live. It's a public statement that you've become a Christian and intend to be one from now on.

WHAT HAPPENS AT BAPTISM

In the earliest days of the Church anyone who decided to be a Christian was baptised straight away, usually in a local river. It was the sign that they belonged both to Jesus and to the Christian community where they lived, and marked them out as 'followers of the way'. From then on their whole life was radically changed.

Water has always been used in Baptism, symbolising both 'washing' and 'drowning'. In the Old Testament there was a ritual washing for any foreigners who wanted to become part of God's people, the Israelites, to show that they'd been cleansed from the evil practices of their previous religion and culture. Centuries later, John the Baptist took this idea but applied it to the Jews themselves, saying that even they needed to repent and be 'made clean' in a visible way. After Jesus' death and resurrection, the Early Church also saw Baptism as a sign that the new believer had died to his former life of sin and risen to new life in Christ. Paul explains this in his letter to the Christians at Rome (6:4): 'we were buried with him through baptism into death in order that . . . we too may live a new life'.

In the Old Testament, God's relationship with his people was based on the promises he made to them, and on what they promised in return. This 'Covenant' was first made with Abraham, and later on the Ten Commandments were part of it. Sadly, the Israelites proved unable to keep their side of the deal, and went their own way, thinking they knew best, but never learning much from their mistakes. In the end, they were overrun by other nations and ended up being exiled to Babylon, the superpower of that time. But God hadn't forgotten his promises, and the Early Church believed strongly that in Jesus he had fulfilled them all; that because of his death and resurrection everyone who lives by faith in him becomes part of the 'New Covenant'. Jesus' words at the Last Supper as he poured out the wine for his disciples make this clear: 'this cup is the New Covenant in my blood, which is poured out for you' (Luke 22:20). Anyone who's baptised therefore comes under the terms of God's New Covenant.

One evening Jesus sat down to have a discussion with a Jewish leader called Nicodemus. He told him that 'unless a man is born again he cannot see the kingdom of God' (John 3:3). It's a great pity that the expression 'born again' has become linked with strange behaviour and way-out American sects. Nothing could have been further from Jesus' mind. He wanted Nicodemus to realise that following him was a decisive and final step, so he used the picture of being born. Just as a new-born baby leaves its mother's womb and enters into a completely different life, so we start a totally new kind of life when we become followers of Jesus. That's why the Baptism service includes the words: 'Baptism is the sign and seal of this new birth'. It's the sign that the new Christian has been washed clean from his sinful ways and has now begun this new life, having 'died' to the old. The seal is God's Holy Spirit, who fills all

Christians with his presence and gives them strength and power to live the Christian life. To be baptised is to acknowledge publicly that you're taking that decisive step and now intend to follow the way of Jesus.

DECISION TIME

When you're baptised the priest asks three questions which you (or your parents and godparents if you're not old enough) have to answer. It's not an exam, and the answers are written out for you, but they're called 'The Decision' because they show that something's been decided.

1. 'I turn to Christ' – In a nutshell, that's what it is to become a Christian. When someone starts talking to you, your reaction is to turn towards them. If you don't, you give the message that you don't want a conver-

sation with them. Turning to face someone establishes a relationship that can then be continued. We might also say that a friend has 'turned to drink', meaning that the person concerned couldn't find a better way of coping with their difficulties. Both those ideas are contained within this answer – we turn to Christ and enter into a continuing relationship with him, and look to him to give us strength to live every day for him.

2. 'I repent of my sins' – When we see God as he really is, and recognise Jesus as his Son, who in dying for our forgiveness and freedom showed how much he loves us, we begin to understand that we need to think again about our lives. To repent is quite literally 'to think again'. We all realise deep down that we aren't perfect; we frequently say and do things we know we shouldn't and wish we hadn't. But repentance is far more than saying sorry to God in case he gets cross with us. It's also more than a long-term New Year's resolution. Through Jesus' death God forgives not just our wrong words and actions, but also the bad attitudes and motives which lie behind them. We have to be honest with ourselves and with God about those things which need to be put

right, recognising that we can't do anything on our own to deal with them, and opening ourselves to receive his forgiveness, power and love.

3. 'I renounce evil' – When we arrive at a roundabout or crossroads in a car, we have to decide which road to take. Once our minds are made up we then 'turn our backs' on all the other possible routes – it's impossible to go in two directions at once! For the first Christians there were many alternative ways to go, different philosophies and religions they could adopt. Even if the twentieth century seems rather irreligious by comparison, a closer look shows just how many choices there are for us, too. People may not take much part in organised religion, but they put their security in all manner of things – ambition, material possessions, the pursuit of happiness, to name just a few. These ways may seem attractive, but they don't lead us to God. Jesus said: 'I am the way, the truth and the life. No one comes to the Father except through me' (John 14:6). One look at a daily newspaper should be enough to convince us that there's a great deal of evil in the world, and however much governments and other institutions try to get rid of it, selfishness, greed and

exploitation will always be with us. To become a Christian is to turn our backs decisively on the alternatives the world offers us, reject everything that's opposed to God's ways, and turn confidently towards Jesus Christ.

These three questions and answers come in a particular order. We're drawn to the Christian faith when we turn to Jesus and enter into a living relationship with him, but when we do that we also recognise that we have to repent of all that's wrong in our own lives and turn our backs on evil. Once Jesus becomes the focus of our lives we can see ourselves and our world in true perspective. Babies can't decide this for themselves, of course, so when they are baptised the parents and godparents make these promises on their behalf – older children and adults make them on their own. But in either case the Church welcomes a new member and promises to play its part in nurturing them into the Christian faith. Just as we're baptised into the Church, so we're then confirmed as part of it. Personal faith and commitment are essential, but always in the context of the Christian community.

This may sound a bit dry and academic, but in reality it's anything but! At the heart of our relationship with God lies an awareness that he loves us. People become Christians for many different reasons, but for all of them the basic motivation is realising that God really does love them. No one can prove love scientifically but we all know it's real. Babies and their mothers don't analyse their love for each other, nor do husbands and wives – that would be a real passion-killer! Instead they demonstrate their love both with words and actions. John wrote to one of the early churches: 'This is love, not that we loved God but that he loved us and sent his Son as an atoning sacrifice for our sins' (1 John 4:10). God couldn't have done more than that to show how much he loves us. We can't 'prove' his love theoretically, but as we respond to it by following Jesus, we experience the reality of it for ourselves.

Even a hundred years ago the majority of babies would have been baptised, but today only a quarter of children receive baptism while they're still infants. Many parents would rather their children made up their own minds about religion when they're old enough to. If you haven't been baptised, for whatever reason, that obviously has to happen before Confirmation. But don't worry – you can be baptised and confirmed in the same service now, and many bishops encourage this. Ask your parish priest to tell you more about it.

Can You Believe It?

What we believe has a huge impact on our lives, even if we don't think about it most of the time. If we buy a tube of toothpaste at the supermarket, we believe it will contain what it says on the packet, even though cream cheese and instant glue also come in tubes! We may believe that driving up the A1 will bring us to Portsmouth, but however sincere our belief it won't be much use when we reach the centre of Edinburgh!

We can't compare these examples directly with Christian belief, but throughout its history the Church has tried to set out what it believes about God, Jesus and the Holy Spirit. The early Christians had to declare what they believed before they could be baptised, and the Baptism service contains a series of three questions which have to be answered by the candidate or their sponsors. No one needs a degree in theology to be a Christian, but it's still vital to make sure that our faith has a secure foundation – there's no point believing something that isn't right or true.

1. 'Do you believe and trust in God the Father who made the world?'

You don't have to be a Christian to believe in God. Many people acknowledge the existence of a superior being without accepting Christianity. But the question asks more than that. It probes into the sort of God we believe in, and what he's like.

We wouldn't be alive but for our parents – we were born because they were there first, and we rely on their care and help as we grow up. We depend in the same way on our Heavenly Father for our human existence. He's our Creator, who made the universe, the world and everything in it, ourselves included, and the whole of life is in his hands. The view from a mountain-top in the Alps or Himalayas can be quite overwhelming in its magnificence; the sea on a stormy day has a power and beauty beyond words; the night sky opens up a universe of unimaginable dimensions to our eyes. By comparison we seem pretty small and helpless. The earth measures 25000 miles around the Equator and its centre is 4000 miles from the surface. It extends 36000 feet below the ocean in the Challenger Deep, while the summit of Everest is 29000 feet above sea level, which leaves you and me as two tiny dots on its surface. Then we realise that the moon is 238000 miles away, and the sun 93 million miles, which makes even the earth, our home, a tiny pinprick in the Milky Way galaxy. Our sun is a fairly small star among 18000 million others in it, while the Milky Way is just one galaxy of stars in the universe! The immensity beyond imagination of the universe and the beauty and wonder of our tiny planet all point us to the One who brought them into being. Most amazing of all, however, is that each one of us matters deeply to him.

Jesus once told a famous parable about a wayward son to give us a picture of just how much God loves us (Luke 15:11-32). The Prodigal Son, as he's usually known, asks for his share of the estate, and his father gives it to him willingly, though he knows what might happen. After spending it all on partying and living it up the son realises there's none left, and his 'friends' are nowhere to be found. The only work he can find is feeding and tending pigs – the worst job any Jew could have! Eventually he comes to his senses and decides to return home. Perhaps he's wondering how his father will react after the way he's behaved, but before he even reaches the front gate his father rushes out to kiss and embrace him. Despite his dirty, bedraggled state he's welcomed home as a son, and that night there's a great party to celebrate his return. That's what God's like with us when we turn to him. We can only come as we are, spoiled by selfishness and sin and battered by the consequences of our weaknesses and failings, but he accepts us as we are, forgives us, welcomes us home and gives us everything we need to live in his presence. Even those with a poor experience of their father have some idea of what a father should be like – and God goes far beyond that in every way. Extraordinary though it may seem, the same God who created the universe and everything in it wants us, small and insignificant as we are, to know him as intimately as we know our parents. Jesus taught us to pray to 'Our Father in Heaven', and just as he trusted him totally, so he wants us to share in that relationship;

to know God as our Heavenly Father and to enjoy his presence and love in our lives day by day.

2. *Do you believe and trust in his Son, Jesus Christ, who redeemed humankind?*

It's not too hard to get along with a god who remains impersonal and remote, who doesn't get in our way or involve himself in our lives – we can believe in him without commitment. But Christians have always believed in a very different kind of God. At the heart of the Christian faith is Jesus Christ – in fact without him it couldn't be the Christian faith at all! Born into an ordinary home in an obscure corner of the mighty Roman Empire, he never received any special education, didn't publish any of his thoughts or teachings, and probably didn't travel outside his native Palestine. He held no senior government or church appointment, and never seemed to mix with important people. On the contrary, he made himself highly unpopular by denouncing the hypocrisy and self-righteousness of the religious leaders of his day, and instead spent much of his time with ordinary folk and society's cast-offs. He was arrested for no good reason (except showing up the authorities in their true light), condemned at a blatantly unfair trial, and killed as a criminal on a Roman gibbet outside Jerusalem. He was just 33 years old.

So why do Christians focus their attention on this extraordinary individual? Jesus was certainly a great teacher, and no one has ever given more profound insights into our human condition or God's purposes. The Gospels record some of the greatest spiritual and moral teaching ever given, including the Sermon on the Mount and many famous parables. This teaching was backed up by Jesus' actions. He went about healing the sick and handicapped, restoring them to a whole new way of life; he provided a picnic meal for 5000 out of a small boy's squashed packed lunch; he even brought people back to life again. His love and compassion, not to mention his integrity and single-mindedness, are widely accepted as an example we'd all do well to follow. But special as these things are, they don't of themselves make Jesus the central point of the Christian faith, though they certainly point us towards that conclusion.

No one is completely happy with themselves. We can appear to be very successful and confident on the surface but too often we try to go it alone without God's help, and succeed only in falling flat on our faces. Sin has scarred our lives as a result, and we can do nothing to extricate ourselves from the mess we're in. So God came to the rescue, knowing it was the only way to bring us back into a relationship with himself – 'God so loved the world that he gave his one and only Son, so that whoever believes in him should not perish but have eternal life' (John 3:16). Jesus' death is the focal point of the Christian faith, the Cross its primary symbol. He suffered and died to defeat all the forces of evil and death and to win for us forgiveness and freedom. We're released from the choking grasp of sin, guilt and death to enjoy a completely new life in his presence. For nearly three decades the Berlin Wall separated the two halves of the city, but the events of 1989 led to it being demolished once and for all. Our sin was like that, a barrier separating us from God, but Jesus' death and resurrection have destroyed what Paul calls the 'dividing wall of hostility' between us and God. There's no longer anything to keep us away from his love.

When a new baby arrives people soon start saying, 'Isn't he like his dad!' or, 'She's the image of her mum!'. Whether or not this is just wishful thinking, children often reflect something of their parents. So too in Jesus we can see something of what our heavenly Father is like – he came to show us

God in a way we'd understand. His death wasn't a tragic end caused by a gross miscarriage of justice, but the culmination of God's plan to save humankind. No film-director could have dreamed up the resurrection as a climactic finale, but then it wasn't a finale at all, and definitely not a 'happy ending'. It's the final chapter in the story of our salvation – without it Christianity wouldn't exist. In the Baptism service the priest asks God's blessing on the water with these words: 'Bless this water, so that . . . who is washed in it may be made one with Christ in his death and resurrection, to be cleansed and delivered from all sin.' That's why Jesus is at the heart of the Christian faith. Only in him can we receive forgiveness and new life.

3. *'I believe and trust in the Holy Spirit, who gives life to the people of God.'*

There's enough evidence in the world around us to make belief in a Creator God a reasonable option; and there's enough historical data to demonstrate the existence in Palestine 2000 years ago of a teacher and miracle-worker called Jesus. Even on that basis many have accepted him as God's Son. But Christians have always believed in the Holy Trinity, one God but three persons. We've thought about two of them, but who's the third? The evidence for the Holy Spirit, who is that third person, is quite different. His existence can't be demonstrated by science or history, but in the experience of every Christian he's as real and personal, and just as much part of God as the Father and the Son. He was present at Creation (Genesis 1:2) and appears throughout the Old Testament. Jesus was conceived by the power of the Holy Spirit, and when he was baptised the same Holy Spirit came to give him power for his ministry. It was God's Spirit who raised him from death.

The prophet Joel foresaw a day when God would 'pour out his Spirit on everyone' (Joel 2:28). Jesus had told the disciples he wouldn't be with them forever, but he promised them the Holy Spirit to enable them to continue the work he'd begun. So on the Day of Pentecost, when Peter and the other disciples experienced the coming of the Holy Spirit so dramatically, they realised that Joel's prophecy was being fulfilled in and through them. They told their hearers that they needed to repent and be baptised for their sins to be forgiven, following which they would receive the gift of the Holy Spirit, God's presence in the lives of his people. Ever since then, Christians have regarded Baptism as the time when the Holy

Spirit comes on someone to make them a child of God.

At Confirmation it's not just the Bishop who confirms you. When he lays his hands on you he asks God to confirm you with his Holy Spirit, to give you strength to live for him day by day. Many of the first Christians made an instant decision to follow the way of Jesus and commit themselves to him, and were then immediately baptised to make public this new commitment. For many of us becoming a Christian is more of a process than an event, and it may take several months or even years before we can say we're 'committed Christians'. Confirmation marks both the end of this process and the beginning of a totally changed life. He shows us Jesus and how much we need him; he plants the seeds of faith within us and enables them to flourish and grow; he gives us strength to serve God and face difficulties for him; he fills us with joy and love, transforming our relationships and our whole way of looking at life. We can't see or 'prove' him, but like the wind we know the Holy Spirit is there by the effect he has on our lives, and the ancient prayer which the Bishop says asks for this to be true in the lives of all those about to be confirmed.

It's one thing to believe a fact or a theory.

We know Australia exists, but unless we visit or have connections with it our knowledge remains academic – it doesn't make any difference to our lives. Believing in something makes all the difference. The questions in the Baptism service, which you answer again at Confirmation, don't ask if you believe there is a God, but whether you believe in and trust him. The Christian faith is just one creed or philosophy among many others unless we accept its truth and live accordingly. When we affirm what we believe at Confirmation, we also acknowledge that we know God is our loving heavenly Father through his Son Jesus Christ, by the power of his Holy Spirit.

<u>Personal Belonging</u>

We all need to know we belong to someone
or something. Almost the first thing a baby
learns is who it belongs to – childcare
experts call it 'bonding'. A child who grows
up not knowing where it belongs or who it
belongs to will become a confused and sad
adult. We often use symbols to show where
we belong – badges, car stickers, ties or
scarves. They all indicate who and what
we're part of. School uniform creates a
sense of community, while football teams
wear distinctive colours not just to be iden-

tified easily – they emphasise that this is a team which functions together. On a personal level most married couples wear rings to symbolise that they belong together because of their love.

Like Baptism, Holy Communion, or the Eucharist as it's often known, is also a symbol of belonging. Whenever we receive the bread and wine we're reminded that we're part both of God's kingdom and of his people, the world-wide community of Christians. The most obvious difference that Confirmation will make to you is that you'll be able to receive the bread and wine from then on for the rest of your life. In the early Church everyone who was baptised, young or old, probably did so, but since the Reformation the Church of England has delayed receiving Communion until a child has reached the 'years of discretion'. In practice this means the time when it has a reasonable understanding of the Christian faith. A growing number of churches do now admit children to Holy Communion before they're confirmed, usually after a suitable course of instruction, but this isn't yet the general rule, and you may well have to wait until you're confirmed to receive the bread and wine. Many Confirmation services now include a Eucharist so that those who've just been confirmed can take part fully for the first time.

Both Baptism and the Eucharist are 'sacraments' – what the 1662 Prayer Book calls 'an outward sign of an inward grace'. It's not just a simple reminder in case we'd forgotten but a visible way of making real to us what God does in the deepest parts of our lives, giving us strength to live in a way which pleases him. The early Christians used to meet regularly in each other's homes for a fellowship meal, during which they would obey Jesus' command and share the bread and wine as an act of worship and love. They remembered Jesus' words at the Last Supper, on the night of his arrest and trial, when he'd shared the bread with his disciples during the Passover meal: 'This is my body, given for you. Do this in remembrance of me.' When the meal was over, he shared the cup of wine with them: 'This cup is the New Covenant in my blood, which is poured out for you' (Luke 22:19-20). Because these first Christians referred to the bread and wine as Jesus' body and blood, they were accused in some places of cannibalism! They didn't always behave too well either, and Paul had to remind the church at Corinth to take part reverently and properly in the Lord's Supper, so that they didn't eat the bread or drink the wine unworthily (1 Corinthians 11:27). Ever since Paul wrote those words Christians have used them as the basis for the Eucharistic or Thanksgiving Prayer, to consecrate the bread and wine and remember Jesus' death and resurrection until his return in glory. In the Alternative Service Book this prayer includes the acclamation said by everyone present: 'Christ has died. Christ is risen. Christ will come again.' It's there to do more than remind us of historical facts – we must never forget their importance for us personally.

We come to God with our praise

The first event in a typical service is the singing of a hymn by the whole congregation. Usually this is a great hymn of praise, enabling us to focus on God before anything else happens. If we think only about our own concerns we'll put everything else out of perspective. First of all we come to worship God and bring him our praises for all he is and all he's done. The rest of the service is set in this context of giving glory to God.

We come to God with our sins and weaknesses

Every time the Eucharist is celebrated, whatever the style of the service, the Confession and Absolution are included. To receive the bread and wine worthily we must first acknowledge before God our sins and failings. Like the Prodigal Son, we don't deserve to come into our Father's presence at all. In the Prayer of Humble Access, often used in the Communion Service, everyone says: 'We are not worthy to gather up the crumbs under your table.' This isn't grovelling humility but an honest recognition that our selfish attitudes, thoughtless words and hurtful behaviour have spoiled our relationships both with God and with other people.

Sometimes we don't recognise we've done wrong, so the Confession which everyone says together asks God to forgive us even for the sins we've ignored, forgotten about or pretended are nothing to do with us. It doesn't matter how bad we think our sin is, because no one is beyond the reach of God's love and forgiveness. The writer of the letter to the Hebrews says, 'Jesus is able to save completely those who come to God through him' (Hebrews 7:25). But that doesn't mean we can then go away and do whatever we like. In the Absolution which follows the Confession we're assured of God's forgiveness and that we'll be 'confirmed and strengthened in all goodness'. God's Spirit living within us gives us the strength not to fall back into our old ways, even though there are inevitably times when we fail him. He's always ready to receive us back again when we turn to him, and helps us to continue in the new life which is ours in Christ.

Jesus once told a parable about a man who was let off a huge debt, but then refused to forgive a friend who owed him a very small amount. In the Alternative Service Book the Peace, which comes just before the Eucharistic Prayer, is more than a quick break in the proceedings or a chance to greet the rest of the congregation. It's the opportunity to make sure we put right any relationships that have gone wrong between ourselves and someone else. We all come to God as forgiven sinners and must be willing to forgive others too. In God's presence we can't pretend to be what we're not, even if others can only see a 'plastic' smile. Our faces don't always reflect our true feelings, but God knows everything about us – the Psalmist writes: 'O Lord you have searched me and you know me. You know when I sit and when I rise; you perceive my thoughts from afar' (Psalm 139:1-2). He knows us better than we know ourselves – fears, anxieties and weaknesses included. But still he wants us to come to his table and share in his heavenly banquet, and as we come to the altar-rail to receive the bread and wine we're reminded that we can only come as we are, and that's how God accepts us.

We come to God with our gifts

When we worship God we don't switch off the rest of our lives – even if we wanted to we couldn't. We worship him with the whole of our lives – hopes and fears, joys and sadnesses, work and leisure. The bread and wine which are brought with the money to the altar sum up all that we are and have. We may think we're incredibly generous but everything we have is given to us by God on trust, abilities and energy included. King David's words form part of the Offertory Prayer, which is said when the gifts are brought to the altar: 'All things come from you and of your own do we give you.' God owes us nothing yet gives us everything. We offer back to him symbols of our love for him and commitment to his kingdom, and we do so gladly because 'the Lord loves a cheerful giver' (2 Corinthians 9:7). The bread and wine are made by crushing corn and grapes. The original produce has been 'killed' to make bread and wine for us to eat. This picture of dying and rising again to new life are the heart of our faith, because just as Jesus died and was raised to new life, so do we in him. Our old life of sin is gone – we've died to it, and are now alive to God in Jesus Christ.

We come to God with our thanks

The Thanksgiving, or 'Eucharistic' Prayer is said by the President on behalf of everyone present, with the congregation joining in at the key points. After it the bread and wine are regarded as 'consecrated', or set apart exclusively for use in worship. They're still bread and wine but represent and become for us the body and blood of Christ, so great care is taken to treat them reverently. In the first part of this prayer, known as the Preface, we thank God and praise him for creating us and giving us new life through his Son Jesus Christ. He alone is worthy of our praise and worship, and they're his by right. Yet Jesus was born just like any other human being, and was in every respect like us. His life was ordinary but at the same time extra-ordinary, while his death and resurrection bring us forgiveness and freedom and new life. Sin and death are forever defeated and now Jesus reigns with his Father in glory. He sends his Holy Spirit on us to assure us we belong to God. So everyone joins together at the end of this section in the words of the Sanctus: 'Holy, holy, holy Lord, God of power and might. Heaven and earth are full of your glory. Hosanna in the highest!'

After this crescendo of praise the President asks the Holy Spirit to make the bread and wine real to us as the body and blood of our Lord Jesus, and continues with the 'Institution Narrative', which recalls Jesus' words to his disciples at the Last Supper, when he broke the bread and shared the cup of wine with them. Our forgiveness and freedom from guilt come as a direct result of Jesus' body and blood being given for us. So everyone then affirms that 'Christ has died' (it's already happened), 'Christ is risen' (he's alive now), and 'Christ will come again' (our hope for the future).

The final part of the prayer sums all this up. We remember Jesus' death on the cross for us, and announce to everyone the truth of his resurrection and ascension until he comes again in glory. We celebrate this regularly as his people by receiving the bread and wine. We ask God to accept our thanks and worship and to fill us with his Spirit and his love, so that the Eucharist isn't a weekly 'fix' to make us feel better but makes a real and visible difference to our daily lives. The whole prayer ends with a great acclamation of praise to our Saviour God.

We come to God with our prayers

Worship isn't an exclusive personal relationship between us and God. His love in our hearts leads to a real concern both for those we know who are suffering, and for the needs of the whole world. Every service has a time when we join together in bringing these situations to God in prayer as part of our worship and in listening to what he's saying to us. The intercessions are normally led by one person, but even if our prayers remain unspoken we can bring them to God in the quiet of our hearts.

We come to God with our commitment

The bread and wine aren't a weekly 'treatment' for our souls, to make us feel better and help us cope with life. In the first part of the Eucharist the focal point is the reading of God's Word and its explanation in the sermon. That's how we're encouraged to learn more of God and his ways, to meditate on the Bible and to think about how it affects our lives day by day. Worship isn't an excuse for putting our minds into neutral! After the congregation have received Communion, everyone prays together: 'Send us out in the power of your Spirit to live and work to your praise and glory.' Only as God's Holy

Spirit gives us strength can we serve God both in our church fellowship and also in our families, neighbourhoods, schools work-places and in the wider world. It doesn't matter if our work feels unglamorous – God will accept whatever we do in his name, whether or not other people notice it or commend it. We don't do it to earn God's love or favour, because he gives us that any-way, without any strings attached. It's not duty but an expression of our love for him and desire to share it with others. We'll always fail if we try to do things in our own strength, but with the Holy Spirit living in us we'll know God's power and strength to do what he calls us to.

Confirmation isn't an obstacle course you have to complete before you can receive Communion, though during your preparation you'll come to a greater understanding of all that God has done for you in Jesus Christ. As you come to receive the bread and wine for the first time, ask God to use the words and actions of the service to speak to you and inspire you, to help you know you belong to him. A lifetime isn't long enough to take all of this in fully, but as you continue in worship, fellowship and service you'll find your faith and love for God growing stronger.

ACTIVE SERVICE

Because everyone needs to belong somewhere, people tend to join together in
'common interest' groups. Whether you
play tennis or the 'cello, make models or
marmalade, keep hamsters or keep fit,
there's a club somewhere full of people who
share your enthusiasm. On a larger scale
there are political parties, organisations for
people suffering from various illnesses and
groups dedicated to helping the homeless,
the unemployed or the starving. Most of them
have some visible means of identification,

too – a particular colour, badge, logo or uniform. Members are normally expected to support the aims of their organisation with their time and money and take part in its activities.

The Church isn't really a club or society in the usually accepted sense, though its members certainly have a common faith. Archbishop William Temple once said that it was 'the only organisation in the world which exists solely for the benefit of its non-members', and while it may seem like a huge institution, the Church throughout the western world has decreased in size dramatically since the Second World War. In the UK today barely 8 per cent of the population go to church at all apart from weddings and funerals, and of these less than 2 per cent attend their local parish church.

When you're confirmed, you're not being put on the select membership list of an exclusive club. Receiving the bread and wine at the Eucharist is an important part of it, because it shows you belong to God. Equally important is that you become an active adult member of God's Church, and belong to all his people throughout the world, though particularly in the Anglican Church. Regrettably, some churches do resemble a closed society, and give the impression that if you haven't achieved a certain social and educational level you won't be accepted. Others seem to look down on anyone who doesn't hurtle from one meeting to the next in a frenzied whirl. Christian commitment certainly isn't identified either by qualifications or etiquette, nor yet by rushing around in ever-decreasing circles. There has to be a proper balance between meditation and reflection on the one hand, which are necessary for spiritual growth, and demonstrating our faith in practical service on the other.

Acts 2 gives us a picture of how the Church was organised in its earliest days. Life's very different now, and it's unrealistic to try and copy this in every detail, but we can draw from it a pattern or framework for church organisation and involvement to help us understand better where we might fit in and what part we might play.

Discipleship

Jesus called his first disciples to follow him and share in his ministry. Over a three-year period they listened to his teaching, saw all that he did, and gradually realised that in him God's plans would come to their ultimate fulfilment. Although they were ordinary people, they had first-hand knowledge and experience of Jesus and all the believers respected them as the apostles. Their authority in the earliest church was based not just on their personal relationship with Jesus but also on their experience of the Holy Spirit at Pentecost. In the same way that the Spirit had come on Jesus at his baptism to confirm his unique status as God's Son and empower him for his ministry, so also he came on the disciples to give their teaching and ministry the authority of God himself, and equip them to serve him. As a result they themselves taught the new believers, emphasising that all who follow the Lord Jesus will also be filled with the Spirit, to assure them that they're God's children, and to give them all the resources they need to live the Christian life. Paul's letters indicate that the Early Church took it as read that this would apply to every believer. In 1 Corinthians 12, for example, he lists some of the gifts of the Holy Spirit which all Christians receive to enable them to play their part in the ministry of the whole Church and serve him in the world. Being a disciple, or a follower of Jesus involves living in this 'power of the Spirit' and using our gifts, not to indulge ourselves but for 'the common good'.

Discipleship means 'following'. We follow

Jesus not just as a good example, but most of all because in him we see the pattern for our own ministry. Ministry isn't restricted to people who are ordained, or those who seem specially holy. The gifts of the Holy Spirit are given to all believers, regardless of status or background. Healing, prophecy, discernment – they're all just as relevant to the Church in the twentieth century as they were in the first, even if they're practised in slightly different ways. They help God's people to grow in worship and love and form the basis of the Church's witness to the world around. To take one example, many churches are rediscovering the ministry of Christian healing, not as a way of bypassing delays in the health service but in order to bring God's wholeness to people's lives as Jesus did. Not everyone has that ministry, but every Church member has some gift. Paul illustrates this by likening Christians to parts of a body, each fulfilling its own distinct function, but contributing to the overall life, health and activity of the body.

Disciples are learners before they're doers, however. The early Christians sat and listened to the apostles' teaching, learning from it just as the disciples themselves had learned from their Master. Rushing around doing lots of things (even if those things are good in themselves) ends in a spiritual cul-de-sac, because no time's been given to listening and learning.

When the Bishop lays his hands on you at Confirmation he prays that you'll be confirmed with the Holy Spirit. This is the heart of the Christian life, where what we believe is demonstrated by the way we live. Read the Bishop's prayer again now, so that when you hear him say those words just before you're confirmed you'll be able to make them real for your life.

Worship

The early Christians were really keen! You just couldn't stop them praying and worshipping. Every day on their way to prayers in the Temple they'd meet together and pray in the outer courtyards. They also met regularly in each other's homes to share a meal and fellowship, learn more about their faith, and obey Jesus' command to commemorate his death and resurrection at the Last Supper by breaking bread together. And they'd praise God anywhere – even in prison, as the jailer at Philippi discovered when Paul and Silas started singing hymns during the night! Although two thousand years have passed since then, and the Church has adapted to innumerable different cultures and circumstances, it has always regarded worshipping God as its central activity.

Worship is the greatest activity we can ever take part in, because as we give God his worth, we become more like God created us to be, more fully human. But the Church at worship is much more than the sum total of its parts. We all bring our individual praises and thanksgiving, but as we celebrate God's love and forgiveness together we find ourselves caught up in something far greater than we could know on our own. The New Testament certainly emphasises our personal relationship with God through Jesus Christ, but it gives equal priority to our corporate life as Christians. We can't live in a spiritual 'bubble' of our own, doing our own thing in isolation from other Christians, because God created us to live in community. So as members of his family we come together regularly to worship him. Sometimes that can be exciting and even emotional, because worship comes from the heart, though the extreme emotionalism that loses its grip on reality is dangerous. At the same time cold, academic or insensitive worship with all traces of emotion removed is hardly preferable. We all express our feelings in different ways but there's nothing wrong with being enthused or excited by our experience of

God, through Jesus Christ in the power of the Holy Spirit. It's a foretaste of heaven where, as Charles Wesley wrote in a famous hymn, we'll be 'lost in wonder, love and praise'.

Fellowship

A football team isn't just made up of eleven talented individuals. If its members are more concerned to show off their own skills than to play together for the good of the whole team, there won't be many trophies in the cabinet. Successful teams are those whose members learn to pull together and play to each other's strengths in order to win the match.

Because Christians belong to God they also belong to one another. One of the most striking features of the Early Church was the way the believers came together and cared for each other, sharing what they had so that no one remained in need. Yes, they had their disputes, as we see from some of Paul's letters, but their overriding aim was to show the love of Jesus in their corporate life. Jesus himself said: 'It is by your love for one another, that everyone will recognise you as my disciples' (John 13:35). His command applies just as much to us. It's a marked contrast with the rest of the world, where the message is 'Do what's right for you'. We don't need to neglect ourselves in a stupid or attention-seeking way, but we have to recognise that our self-interest often causes misery or suffering to others. Our fellowship must display the hallmarks of God's love and its effect on our relationships.

Stewardship

C. S. Lewis once said that Christian giving only starts when it hurts us! Most people will put a small amount in the collection plate or Christian Aid envelope, but the first Christians went far beyond that – they were even willing to sell their possessions so that they could provide for those in greater need than their own. There wasn't a gap between the 'haves and the have-nots'. But by the time James wrote his letter, he was having to criticise churches where the well-heeled were given the best seats while the poor had to stand at the back (James 2:1-4). Whatever we have in the way of possessions or bank-balances is given us by God on trust. We've no right to flaunt our wealth or assume it bestows a higher status on us. It's to be used in God's service, not to buy privilege or indulge ourselves at the expense of others.

In the Old Testament God's people paid a tithe. Ten per cent of all they had they gave back to God to be used both for maintaining the Temple and also for the benefit of the whole community, especially the poor and vulnerable.

When we give money to God's work, we're not just giving it to the Church or some other organisation. First of all we're offering back to God a small part of what he's given us, not just money, but also the time and energy and ability that's gone into producing it. God's generosity knows no limits. In turn we give as generously as possible of what we can offer; nothing's so small that God can't use it. As Paul told the Christians at Corinth, 'the Lord loves a cheerful giver' (2 Corinthians 8:7).

Leadership

Football teams have captains or managers, schools have headteachers, and countries have monarchs or presidents. Leaders are necessary for any group of people to work together, large or small. We often think of Church leaders in terms of bishops and archbishops, dressed up in their robes looking like a production of *The Mikado*! In fact, many of their duties don't require them to dress up. Their work covers a large area of responsibility, as well as a huge geographical area. That's why each parish has a leader too, called a vicar or rector; sometimes he or she will have a curate working for them if the parish is large enough. Unfortunately leaders of all sorts sometimes become very dictatorial and power-hungry, and Church leaders have also fallen into this trap at times. But the standard for Christian leadership is very clear – all authority comes from God and can only be exercised under his control. Jesus invariably spoke and acted on his Father's authority, even though many said: 'He speaks as one who has authority.' His disciples were amazed when he knelt and washed their feet – only the lowest servant would have done such a menial job. Christian leaders aren't there to order the congregation about or make everyone 'dance to their tune'. Their main task is to act as servants in Jesus' name, which doesn't preclude them from taking responsibility or making decisions, but shows them how to go about it.

One day Jesus' disciples were squabbling over their status, so he gently put them straight by saying: 'whoever wants to be great among you must be your servant, and whoever wants to be first must be the willing slave of all. For the Son of Man did not come to be served but to serve, and to give his life as a ransom for many' (Mark 10:43-45).

Even if leadership in the Church is focused

on one or two individuals, we all share in it. That includes respecting those who make decisions and bear the most responsibility, rather than criticising what they do. We can share their burden by praying for them, and help them by making sure we do whatever's required of us.

When Paul wrote his letters to the Christians at Corinth he had to tell them off because the Church there was riddled with disputes. Instead of using their gifts and resources for everyone's benefit they were showing off and arguing, and causing needless trouble. Some gifts may be more public than others, but in God's eyes all are equal. The Holy Spirit lives in every Christian and gives him or her gifts, not for self-indulgence but to build up God's people so that together they can serve him, which is the basic driving force behind all Christian ministry.

LOOK ALIVE

During the winter months many plants can seem completely dead. Only a brown twig sticking out of the ground indicates that anything might be there, but if you look closely you'll see the tiny buds which in spring will burst into leaf. A mother knows her baby is alive long before it's born from the kicks and bumps inside her, and when it finally arrives it makes a lot of noise too! We know when things are alive because they move, grow, develop and react to their environment.

Spiritual life can be identified in the same way. As Christians we grow and develop, and respond to our world in a Christian way. It should be obvious to those around us that we're Christians, whether they're friends, family or people we meet only occasionally. A witty little poster shows a little monk standing in a courtroom, obviously on trial – the caption reads: 'If you were on trial for your faith, would there be enough evidence to convict you?'

Relationships

The clearest evidence comes in the way we conduct our personal relationships, and few things cause us more headaches than how we get along with other people. Even the happiest of families will have an occasional flare-up, and the most devoted lovers the odd tiff. Neighbours fall out with each other, rival groups of football supporters spoil for a brawl, while nations go to war over a territorial dispute. Conflict is close to the heart of our human nature, a fact which most great writers have used in their plays or novels, as they describe the complexities of human relationships and the disasters which follow when they break down and fall apart.

Becoming a Christian won't resolve all

your problems with other people overnight. There'll always be conflicts and strife while human beings exist, and we can't escape them. But the Christian faith does start to make a difference – in you! You don't need to wear rose-coloured spectacles, or develop a convenient blindness to everyone's faults, but as you allow God's love to fill your life, you'll become more compassionate and caring. You'll be more willing to listen than to shout; to understand than to criticise; to put other people's interests ahead of your own. The Church has many detractors who are only too ready to point out its faults and ignore its good points. Sometimes their criticisms are valid, but Christians have often had a positive effect on relationships and people-issues. St Francis led the way in his generation in caring for the poor and looking after God's creation. Lord Wilberforce fought almost single-handed for the abolition of slavery. Mother Teresa has shown God's love by helping countless homeless people in Calcutta; Jackie Pullinger by enabling many to escape from gangs, drug addiction and poverty in Hong Kong; Desmond Tutu by bringing reconciliation between those who hated each other in South Africa. They're all ordinary people like us, who've achieved amazing things for God's kingdom simply by following his leading and sharing his love. In fact, when those who claim to be Christians provoke bitterness and strife, or encourage division and hostility, we start to wonder how genuine their faith really is. God doesn't ask us to like everyone – instead he commands us to love them, which is infinitely more demanding, and only possible because of the love of Jesus within us. If we start among our own family and friends, who knows where it might end?

At school or college

Being a Christian in church isn't too hard. At least everyone expects it there. They'll be pleased you want to be confirmed and encourage you to express your faith in word and action. You won't need to stand up for what you believe in. Elsewhere it's rather different. Your friends may well think it's not 'cool' to be 'religious', and you may be tempted to keep your beliefs to yourself. But if they're behaving in a way you feel you can't as a Christian you'll probably want either to challenge what they're doing or keep well away from it. That may make them a bit uncomfortable, and you won't necessarily be too popular. You might even wonder at times if the cost of being a Christian is too high. But you'd be surprised how much you can achieve with God's help. Perhaps you could get alongside someone who's being bullied or victimised; you could avoid malicious gossip and spreading rumours, making sure you only say what you know to be true; you could give a bit more support to that charity collection; you could condemn drug-taking or casual sexual relationships. Not all the issues are so cut-and-dried, but if you show integrity and compassion in all you do (homework included!), you'll find it counts for a very great deal.

Opinions

Most of us like airing our views on everything from politics to car maintenance. We inevitably form opinions on most issues, especially those which affect us directly. Unfortunately, we don't always check our information too well, and what we say can often be affected by our own prejudices. Being a Christian won't give us all the relevant facts, and it certainly doesn't entitle us to assume that whatever we say is automatically right! But our worship and prayer, and day by day relationship with God should have some effect on our personal opinions. Not that we'll always agree with other people, even other Christians – there are Christian politicians in all the major parties, who hold different views on how to run the country but still join together as Christians to share and express their faith. The Holy Spirit doesn't supply us with simple answers to all the world's problems, but if he fills our hearts and minds certain things will follow:

i) We'll be willing to listen to other people's views and express our own with sensitivity.

ii) We'll try not to jump to hasty conclusions based on our own prejudices, but instead think carefully before taking sides.

iii) We'll be less judgmental of those who don't see things our way.

iv) We'll take action based on our views – it's no use condemning the plight of the homeless if we do nothing to help them ourselves.

Evangelism

Perhaps this word gives you the shivers. It smacks of well-heeled American preachers persuading gullible people to part with their money, or of persistent callers at the front door while you're trying to eat your evening meal. It's a pity that these people have given evangelism a bad name, because it's not about manipulating people in order to raise more funds, nor even about getting new recruits for the church. Rather, it's a way of life to which all Christians are called so that others can experience God's love and grace for themselves, and enter into a living relationship with him through Jesus Christ. The way we live and behave will say just as much about this as our words – clever talking may impress for a while, but it won't bring anybody to faith, and haranguing people is a guaranteed way of putting them off!

If you've 'nailed your colours to the mast' it may well provoke questions about your faith and give you the opportunity to answer them. Evangelism isn't a sales pitch. You should be courteous and open in all conversations, as willing to listen as to speak. But don't be ashamed of your faith either – if you're not convinced it's for real, you're not likely to convince anyone else.

Conflict

In the Western world there's little direct opposition to Christianity. Religious tolerance is the order of the day, and we'd be appalled if anyone was beaten up or tortured because of their personal beliefs. But there are plenty of more subtle kinds of opposition – ridicule, rejection or even anger. We shouldn't be too surprised at this. Jesus aroused great controversy and hostility, so much that he was eventually killed as a criminal. Just before his arrest he said: 'If the world hates you, keep in mind that it hated me first' (John 15:18). As followers of Jesus we can expect such reactions at times. People may dismiss our beliefs as quaint or naive; going to church regularly may exclude us from some other Sunday activities such as sport; we may even arouse anger by making a stand, and find people saying things about us which are unkind or untrue. It was far worse for the first Christians, but Peter wrote to some of them saying that by living the Christian life they could 'greatly rejoice, even though now for a little while you may have had to suffer grief in all kinds of trials' (1 Peter 1:6). We can't experience anything Jesus hasn't been through before us, and the Holy Spirit will give us the strength and courage to cope with it, come through it, and carry on serving God.

Confirmation is about receiving the Holy Spirit, and Paul told the Galatian Christians that their lives must bear 'the fruit of the Spirit'. While we won't achieve perfection this side of Heaven, there should be some kind of evidence that our lives are being changed each day by the Holy Spirit. Other people should begin to see a radical difference in our lives, whether or not things are going well. Christians aren't exempt from sadness, anxiety or conflict – Jesus endured all of these. The difference is in the way they affect us and the way we respond.

Being a Christian isn't an easy option. It's more like a battle, as we're reminded in the Baptism service. Paul told the Christians at Ephesus that we need 'spiritual armour' from God to help us in the battle (Ephesians 6:10-20). But we shouldn't be discouraged. Jesus said to his disciples, 'Take heart! I have overcome the world' (John 16:33). Jesus came to defeat the forces of evil once and for all, and by sharing his risen life we also share in his victory over them. When you declare your faith at Confirmation you're going in with your eyes open, knowing the consequences of following Jesus; you also know his Holy Spirit within you will equip you to face them.

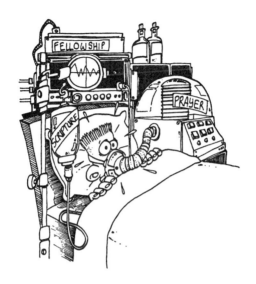

THE LIFE-SUPPORT SYSTEM

Baptism and Confirmation are both about belonging – to God our Father, and to his family, the Church. We can't be Christians in isolation, and need the fellowship of other believers for support and encouragement. At the same time, we have to learn to 'stand on our own two feet'. An astronaut walking in space or on the moon would die without a vast range of back-up assistance, both in his spacecraft and back on earth. But he also needs his own life-support system.

Daily prayer, meditation and Bible reading are the Christian's life-support system. We don't have to wait for the next church service or meeting to renew our relationship with God, because prayer gives us direct access to him. Since he's always with us by his Spirit we can speak to him as often as we want.

Reading the Bible

Why bother reading each day from a book ranging from two to three thousand years old? There are plenty of great works of literature, philosophy or science which everyone agrees are masterpieces, but no one reads them for private devotion. So what makes the Bible different and special?

We've already seen how creation reveals something of God's character to us, but Christians believe the Bible teaches us even more about him. In it we read not just about Creation, but also the history of his people, the prophets, Jesus himself, and the life of the Early Church. We see God in action among his people, and on a deeper level recognise him at work in our own lives and circumstances.

The Bible's a complicated book, made up of sixty-six smaller books written over a long period in a very different culture from our own. It's not always an easy book to understand, and to start with you'll probably need to find some help. The Church of

England, for example, has a 'lectionary', a system of reading it which makes sure we don't just concentrate on our favourite bits. That's fine for churches, but not so practical for personal use, so you could consider buying an inexpensive basic guide to the Bible's various books, themes and characters, to give you an overall picture. Many Christians also make use of daily Bible-reading notes, such as those produced by the Bible Reading Fellowship, Scripture Union or 'Every Day with Jesus'. These are meant to be devotional rather than scholarly and help to get you into a daily habit of Bible-reading by explaining it in simple terms and applying it to everyday life. It won't all make sense at first, and you shouldn't worry if some parts of the Old Testament seem a bit obscure, or Paul's letters don't speak deeply to you. There'll also be many times when the words leap off the page at you, making sense of what's happening in your life. Don't be surprised either if the Bible makes you feel uncomfortable occasionally, or challenges you to a particular course of action. There are plenty of misconceptions about the Bible, and many people dismiss it as fairy-tales, or the product of a different age and culture which has no relevance today. But by approaching it with an open heart and mind, the Holy Spirit will reveal its meaning for you, and you'll find there's no end to its riches.

Although there are many good reasons for reading the Bible as literature or history, Christians don't just read it for background information or moral guidance. First and foremost it's God's Word to us, and in its pages we hear him speaking, revealing more of his will both for us and the world. Above all it's through God's written word that we encounter his Living Word, Jesus himself, and recognise him as a quite unique person, whose integrity bore out his claims about his relationship with his heavenly Father. All Christians go through times when they don't feel like reading the Bible, or can't make much sense of it, which is why making it a daily habit is so important. God is worthy of our praise and worship all the time, not just when we feel like it. If our hearts and minds are open to him, we'll discover all kinds of new insights by persevering with the Bible, and even if we don't understand everything we read, often a phrase or idea will stay with us to deepen our love for God and strengthen our faith in him.

Talking to God – and listening

Good relationships are based on good communications. Boyfriends and girlfriends who never talk to each other don't stay together for very long, and friendships don't last if there are no letters, phone calls or visits. In our conversations we communicate to the other person our thoughts and feelings and learn more about them – the more we communicate with someone else, the better we get to know them. That leads to greater trust and confidence in the relationship, especially when there's a crisis.

It's the same in our relationship with God. The more we speak with him and listen to him, the closer it becomes. He doesn't just want to hear from us when things are going wrong, but also when we're happy and thankful, or want his guidance in a particular situation. He never turns us away and understands exactly how we feel, whether we're finding prayer a joy or a struggle. All great Christians have made a habit of prayer – Martin Luther once said he had so much to do that he'd never get it done if he didn't pray for three hours first! And there are no fixed rules because it's not a technique but a relationship. Here are a few thoughts:

i. *Prayer is focusing on God.* When we look through the viewfinder of a camera our eye is drawn to the subject, which we then focus on until we can see it clearly. As we make

God the centre of our focus and attention we forget about ourselves and concentrate on his glory and power, his love and mercy, his compassion and forgiveness. We're often miserable because we think too much about ourselves. By focusing on God we discover that our own situation comes more clearly into perspective, too.

ii. *Prayer is entering God's will.* We can never 'bend God's ear' to get him to see things our way! Prayer isn't for the closed mind that's already decided what God should do. On the contrary, it means opening our minds and wills to him, letting him change our attitudes and thoughts so that we see things more as he sees them. We won't always see God's will clearly, and at times we'll be tempted to go our own way, but even if he only shows us the next stage of the journey we know he'll give us all we need to get through it. Sometimes in praying for people and situations we may be aware of God speaking specifically to us, helping us to pray in line with his will. After all, he knows and hears our prayers even before we've prayed them.

iii. *Prayer is committing ourselves to God.* By focusing on God and entering his will, we're committing ourselves to his ways, whatever the cost. God dislikes nothing more than apathy and lack of commitment. Prayer is simple yet profound, easy yet demanding of our time and energy. Faith always leads to action – it's no use praying for poor old Mrs Jones who's lonely and housebound if we're not prepared to pay her a visit or help her out. Our prayers and faith have to be seen in the way we live and act day by day. When we pray for the world or even a small part of it, we're acknowledging our part in God's purposes to increase his kingdom of love.

iv. *Prayer is believing God will act.* There'd be no point in praying if God did nothing. He'd be either powerless or simply callous! We bring our concerns to God in faith, believing he'll both hear us and act on our requests. Not that he'll give us whatever we ask for – as our loving Father he gives us what he knows is best, even if at times we don't really understand why things have turned out the way they have. God asks us to trust him and leave the results in his loving and strong hands. Much as we hate giving up control, it's a vital part of our prayer life.

v. *Prayer is being renewed each day.* Renewal isn't something that only happens when you become a Christian or have a particular experience. The Christian life is a constant process of being changed. In prayer we open ourselves to God's love and power and to his Holy Spirit, asking for fresh guidance and new spiritual vitality. Often it's in the moments of greatest need that we learn most about God's love and care, and as we experience it our faith grows deeper. Like the Psalmist we discover his power to 'reach down and take hold' of us, transforming our despair into hope and filling us with the joy of his Spirit. It's a long, slow process and we make many mistakes on the way – it's only when we look back that we realise how far God has brought us.

vi. *Prayer is enjoying God's presence.* It's sometimes hard to take in, but the most important part of prayer is relaxing and enjoying God's presence! Just as the Prodigal Son arrived home to a party in his honour, little though he deserved it, that's how it should be when we come to God.

Ideas for approaching prayer

Be yourself – There's no point pretending to be what we're not, and papering over the cracks, because God knows us better than we know ourselves, and accepts us with all our faults and failings. In his presence we can be fully ourselves.

Be quiet – We can't listen properly if we're still talking. It's important to be quiet so that we can hear God's 'still, small voice' and experience his peace in a noisy, confusing world.

Be open – If we hold on to prejudices and wrong attitudes we're shutting out the Holy Spirit from our lives. God wants to change us for the better, but he can't if we're not open to him.

Be simple – God doesn't demand long words or a theology degree, and doesn't give our prayers a score for their length or complexity. The prayer Jesus taught his disciples isn't wordy or involved, but it's the most profound of all prayers. We can pray using whatever words come naturally to us and as the Holy Spirit guides us.

Be imaginative – Why get stuck with words at all? We can just as easily picture the situation we're bringing to God in our mind's eye, and see how it develops. That might be part of God's answer!

Be thankful – Gratitude to God should be the recurring theme of every prayer; he's given us so much to be thankful for and rejoice in. Remembering to say thank you also stops us complaining too much!

Even if your prayers don't seem to be 'getting through' and just bouncing back off the ceiling, God's not keeping a record of how well you're doing – he knows when circumstances or feelings make it seem difficult to spend time reading and praying. But without the habit of daily Bible reading and prayer the Bishop's prayer from Isaiah 11 in the Confirmation service can't be answered. God's Spirit only comes on us when we turn to him.

THE CONFIRMATION SERVICE

You may be wondering why Confirmation is necessary at all. Nowhere is it mentioned in the Bible, and the Early Church didn't practise it in the way we do. Baptism, on the other hand, is spoken of frequently in the New Testament, and appears at first sight to be the more important rite. So if any priest can administer Baptism, why do we need a Bishop for Confirmation.

Approaching Confirmation

In the Early Church, you became a Christian and were baptised almost at the same time;

you would then receive the Holy Spirit by the laying on of hands. Only later did these events become widely separated in time. Many children died in infancy, so people wanted them baptised as soon as possible. As time went on Bishops were taking responsibility for larger and larger areas (called dioceses), and rarely could they be present at a Baptism to lay their hands on the person concerned. After the Reformation, the Church of England in effect turned Confirmation into a rite for teenagers to enable them to 'confirm' the faith their parents and godparents had professed on their behalf at baptism. Beforehand, the candidates had to learn the basis of the Christian faith (the Catechism) which then formed part of the service.

We've now returned to something like the practice of the Early Church by providing a service which includes Baptism, Confirmation and a Eucharist, presided over by a Bishop. Those who come to faith as adults are baptised and confirmed at the same time and immediately become full members of the Church and are able to receive the bread and wine. Not all Confirmations take place in such a service, and many are still confirmed having been baptised as infants, so it's quite possible for Confirmation to have a service to itself, without Baptism or the Eucharist. If you've not yet been baptised, that must happen before you're confirmed and should ideally be performed by the Bishop at the same service. It works exactly as for babies, except that parents and godparents aren't in evidence. If you were baptised as a baby, then you'll have to renew your baptismal promises, which you do as part of being confirmed. Whatever the particular service in which your Confirmation takes place, the rite itself remains exactly the same.*

RENEWAL OF BAPTISMAL VOWS

The candidates stand before the Bishop; he says

You have come here to be confirmed. You stand in the presence of God and his Church. With your own mouth and from your own heart you must declare your allegiance to Christ and your rejection of all that is evil. Therefore I ask these questions:

Do you turn to Christ?
Answer **I turn to Christ.**

Do you repent of your sins?
Answer **I repent of my sins.**

---

* The wording of the Confirmation Service given here is taken from the Church of England's Alternative Service Book (1980). The Service may vary slightly in wording throughout the worldwide Anglican Church.

Do you renounce evil?
Answer   **I renounce evil.**

Then the Bishop says

You must now declare before God and his Church that you accept the Christian faith into which you were baptised and in which you will live and grow.

Do you believe and trust in God the Father, who made the world?
Answer   **I believe and trust in him.**

Do you believe and trust in his Son Jesus Christ, who redeemed mankind?
Answer   **I believe and trust in him.**

Do you believe and trust in his Holy Spirit, who gives life to the people of God?
Answer   **I believe and trust in him.**

The Bishop turns to the congregation and says

This is the faith of the Church.
All   **This is our faith.**
         We believe and trust in one God,
         Father, Son and Holy Spirit.

THE CONFIRMATION

The Bishop stands before those to be confirmed and says

Our help is in the name of the Lord
All   **Who has made heaven and earth.**

Blessed be the name of the Lord
All   **Now and for ever. Amen.**

The Bishop stretches out his hands towards them and says

Almighty and everliving God,
you have given your servants new birth
in baptism by water and the Spirit,
and have forgiven them all their sins.
Let your Holy Spirit rest upon them:
the Spirit of wisdom and understanding;
the Spirit of counsel and inward strength;
the Spirit of knowledge and true godliness;
and let their delight be in the fear of the
Lord.
Amen.

The Bishop lays his hand on the head of each candidate, saying

Confirm, O Lord, your servant *N* with your Holy Spirit.

and each one answers
Amen.

After confirmation, the Bishop invites the people to join with him and say

**Defend, O Lord, your servants
with your heavenly grace,
that they may continue yours for ever,
and daily increase in your Holy Spirit
more and more,
until they come to your everlasting
kingdom.
Amen.**

The four elements of the Confirmation

1. The Baptismal vows are confirmed by the candidates

This is particularly for those who were baptised as infants and who are now making those promises for themselves. Those who've been baptised just previously may feel as though they're in for a 500-mile service! However, it reinforces the importance both of becoming a Christian and of believing in the Christian faith. Confirmation has always been inextricably linked with Baptism.

2. *The Confirmation Prayer is said by the Bishop*

Before he does, however, he announces to the congregation that 'Our help is in the name of the Lord', to which they reply, 'who has made heaven and earth'. The responses at this point are more than just a warning that the Confirmation itself is about to start. They also serve to focus our attention away from what's happening towards God, through whom alone it's possible.

The prayer itself is very ancient and based very closely on Isaiah 11. It's a prayer specifically for the candidates, who will normally be standing or kneeling in front of the Bishop by this stage. Its words stress again the fact that new birth and forgiveness are the basis of becoming a Christian, and the importance of Baptism in this. From now on, the candidates are going to live the Christian life publicly, and they'll only do this in the power of God's Holy Spirit, whom the Bishop asks God to send upon them. He prays for three aspects of receiving the Spirit and living in his strength:

Understanding: We all have to continue to grow in our understanding of Christianity, not just as an intellectual exercise, but much more as a way of helping us to grow as Christians and recognise how our faith contributes to our everyday life.

Strength: We need God's help day by day to face all the challenges and difficulties of being a Christian in a sometimes hostile environment.

Spirituality: We grow more and more to be like Jesus as we seek God's will and try to serve him. God doesn't just want us to do things for him. He wants us to take time to enjoy his presence, to pray and meditate, and to live more and more in a way which pleases him.

We won't always succeed – in fact we'll fail far more often than we'd want – but as we look back we'll be able to see how far God has brought us and how he's helped us.

3. *The Bishop lays hands on each candidate*
The candidate kneels in front of the Bishop, asking that the Holy Spirit will confirm each one. This is the Confirmation itself. It sets the seal on all that God has done for each individual up to this point, and as they're confirmed with the Holy Spirit, so they're in a sense being 'sent out' to live the Christian life.

4. *The congregation joins the Bishop in praying for the candidates*

The prayer stresses the forward-looking element of Confirmation, requesting God to defend those who've been confirmed and keep them in himself, and help them to grow daily in his Spirit until they come to be with him for ever. If the Eucharist is to follow, the Peace will be shared at this point, a practical sign that the candidates can now share the bread and wine at 'the Lord's table'.

The significance of the service

What is Confirmation for? There are all sorts of views on this question, but most of them would fit under one of the following descriptions:

- It expresses Christian commitment. Those who are confirmed are making a clear stand for the Christian faith, and publicly affirming their own turning to Christ, repentance for their sins and rejection of evil.

- It is an occasion when the Holy Spirit is received in a conscious way. The Confirmation Prayer brings this out and highlights why the Spirit is a vital part of our walk with God.

- Confirmation provides a connection between Baptism and the Eucharist, and the service which includes all three brings us more into line with the practice of the Early Church.

- It looks forward to the life which those confirmed will now live in the strength of the Holy Spirit. The candidates are being sent out to live as Christians in the world.

- It affirms that the candidates belong to the worldwide Anglican Church.

- Confirmation may feel like an end in itself, but it's only the end of stage one of the journey.

A QUESTION OF FAITH

The most influential and convincing Christians are usually the most thoughtful ones. Being a Christian doesn't mean 'kissing your brains good-bye' or 'rolling your marbles down the aisle'! Christianity which isn't based on prayer, meditation and careful thinking is bound to be pretty superficial – the surface may look impressive but there's not much underneath it. Here are a few questions for you to think through. They're not an end-of-term test but are designed to help you think more deeply about what you believe and how you live as a Christian. You can try answering them for yourself in a quiet moment, or if you're in a preparation group why not raise some of the issues with the other members? Whatever happens these questions are too important to ignore:

1. Does Baptism make you a Christian? Does it make any difference at all?

2. Is becoming a Christian a one-off event or a long process? What makes someone decide to be a Christian?

3. Does it still matter what we believe about God, Jesus or the Holy Spirit? Has science enabled us to get rid of some traditional beliefs?

4. Is it acceptable for Christians to disagree? Are there some things they have to agree about?

5. How important is it to receive the bread and wine at Communion regularly?

6. What gifts has the Holy Spirit given you to serve God in the Church and the world? How will you make use of them?

7. What's the most important part of worship for you?

8. Why do you prefer a particular style of worship? Why do you respond to it where others might be left cold?

9. What are the biggest challenges you face as a Christian in your family, at school or at college?

10. How and when do you find it easiest to read the Bible and pray?

11. What's your main reason for being confirmed?

12. What effect will Confirmation have on your life?

TAKE THE PLUNGE

Before he can jump out of an aircraft safely, a parachutist has to be properly trained and equipped. He must know how his parachute works and how to operate it correctly; he needs to learn how to land without breaking a leg; he must find out where he's supposed to land so that he jumps at the right time; he may also work out the height and speed of the aircraft. All this is interesting but rather academic – unless he actually gets to the point where he leaps out into space and pulls the ripcord! He needs to take the plunge. The same is true of a diver – however much he knows about the theory of diving and however much he may train in the gym to get his body fit, if he doesn't leap into the water it will all be useless.

It's important that you're properly prepared for being confirmed – it isn't something to undertake lightly. You should have a basic idea of the Christian faith; you may learn a great deal about the Bible and the Church; you may have all sorts of gifts and abilities, but if you don't use them they count for nothing. Like the parachutist or the diver, you have to take the plunge and live the Christian life for real! You don't need a divinity degree to be a Christian and you don't have to undergo special training – Christianity isn't just for specialists!

It may be that you've already decided to be confirmed, but you could well still be thinking on it. Inevitably, there are certain pressures on you to say 'yes' or 'no'. Your local church will be delighted, your family may also be very pleased (though that won't be true for everyone) and your friends may be pleased if you're confirmed with them. Other people may try to deter you. All these things will affect you, but the decision is yours alone. There are always reasons for putting it off – you can never be quite sure what you're letting yourself in for, or what other people may think of you. But you aren't doing it for your family, or even for the Church. You're making this public statement about your faith in God through Jesus Christ to demonstrate your commitment to his ways and determination to live in a way which pleases him. It's him you're following. He loved you enough to send his Son to this earth to live and die for you. He accepts you just as you are and offers you his forgiveness and love, without any conditions at all. He's promised you his Holy Spirit to guide you and help you every day and give not just the strength you need to serve God but a lot more besides! Your commitment to him is your expression of your love for him, and when you declare it publicly at Confirmation, you're telling the rest of the world what he means to you.

After you've read this book, perhaps there will be Confirmation to follow – if there is, you'll discover for yourself that it's both an end and a beginning. It's the end of stage one of your faith journey, but the start of a new life in the power of the Spirit. It won't be easy. You'll have plenty of hurdles to jump, and there will be times when you'll feel like giving up. The Christian life never stops, however. There are many decisions to take after Confirmation, many more points of commitment and recommitment, and many more times when you'll have to take the plunge. If you trust God to hold on to you, he'll never let you go – his hands will always keep you. If there *is* Confirmation to follow, you can be certain that there's a whole new life to follow Confirmation.

Now You're Confirmed
SUSAN SAYERS

Where now? Is that *it*? Of course not. You are starting out on an exciting and challenging adventure that will last for the rest of your life.

Susan Sayers helps you to explore your faith. Looking at aspects such as prayer (where should I pray and how does God actually answer my prayers?), the Bible (where is the best place to start reading it?) and forgiveness (how do I deal with sin?), she will lead you through the many questions, problems and difficulties that Christians encounter, to bring you into a closer relationship with God.